Original title:
The Heartfelt Journey

Copyright © 2024 Creative Arts Management OÜ
All rights reserved.

Author: Violet Murphy
ISBN HARDBACK: 978-9908-0-1074-8
ISBN PAPERBACK: 978-9908-0-1075-5

When Hearts Become Compass Points

Two hearts set sail on a map,
They navigate love's silly gap.
With laughter as their guiding star,
They end up lost at a taco bar.

Each twist and turn brings a new laugh,
The compass spins and takes a half.
They follow crumbs from chips and dip,
On this wild and wobbly trip.

The Odyssey of Connected Souls

Two souls embark on quests bizarre,
With GPS that runs on a jar.
They trip on paths of giggles and sighs,
Waving at squirrels in disguise.

They share the tales of their blunders,
Like dodging ducks in rain-soaked thunders.
Together they wander, both lost and found,
In a world where joy knows no bound.

Stories Carried by the Wind

Whispers of laughter swirl around,
As stories float on the breeze profound.
With kites of dreams that dance and twirl,
They chase the gusts, each laugh a pearl.

The wind tells tales of silly falls,
Of mud-stained jeans and bouncy balls.
Each gust a chance to spread joy wide,
As they run with hearts open, side by side.

Beneath the Canopy of Kindred Spirits

Under trees where shadows play,
Two friends share secrets, come what may.
They snack on fruits, tossed from above,
Laughing out loud with a spark of love.

Their hearts intertwined, tied in a knot,
As squirrels perform tricks on the spot.
They swap stories of days gone by,
Finding joy in every goofy try.

The Silent Symphony of Togetherness

In a world where silence hums,
We dance with socks, not drums.
Cupcakes flying, laughter springs,
Who knew that joy could have no strings?

Our mismatched shoes, a true delight,
We prance around both day and night.
With giggles echoing through the halls,
A symphony of love, it never stalls.

Bridges Built on Dreams

We built a bridge of marshmallow fluff,
Stretched it over waters—kind of tough.
With each silly step, we giggled loud,
Our dreams floated high, and we felt so proud.

But when the wind blew, oh what a sight!
Our bridge collapsed, a fluffy fright.
Yet through the mess, we had a ball,
Merging our dreams, we'd never fall.

Flames of Hope Along the Way

We carried matches, lit them bright,
In hopes of warming up the night.
But instead, we sparked a tiny blaze,
Jumping around in a frantic craze!

With marshmallows toasted on our heads,
We laughed while thinking of new beds.
Flames flickered with dreams galore,
In every jest, we'd found much more.

Rainbows Cast After Storms

After the rain, we donned bright shoes,
Splashing in puddles, all with great hues.
Colors swirling, a nonsense race,
Each droplet held joy, not a trace.

As rainbows arched over our heads,
We danced like we had no threads.
Laughing at clouds that rolled on by,
We'd brighten the gloom, oh my, oh my!

Radiance of Untraveled Paths

A curious cat took a stroll,
With sunglasses stuck on its roll.
It danced past a baker with pies,
Chasing butterflies high in the skies.

At each corner, a chicken would cross,
Unable to find what it had lost.
The road was paved with gum and cream,
Somehow, it felt like a wild dream.

With flip-flops squeaking and laughter loud,
They crafted a mischief, attracting a crowd.
From missteps and slips, giggles arose,
These clumsy antics, the best of shows.

Joyful journeys with friends by your side,
Each twist and turn, a thrilling ride.
A quest for biscuits, or maybe a treat,
Life's little giggles can't be beat!

Reflections on the River of Life

A duck in a boat thought he was a swan,
Singing off-key from dusk until dawn.
He quacked to the fish, thought he'd be a star,
But they just splashed back, 'We don't drive a car!'

The river was wide, with laughter and cheer,
As frogs on a log raised their glasses of beer.
They toasted the brave who dared to float,
While a turtle just yawned and savored his coat.

A squirrel on a raft held tight to some nuts,
While grinning, he told tales of the great winter huts.
With each gentle wave, the stories just flew,
Life's just a party when you're merry and true!

So dance down the current, embrace silly fates,
With friends made of feathers, and food on your plates.
When all seems afloat in chaos supreme,
Just paddle along; it's all just a dream!

A Journey Through the Echoing Silence

A llama decided to take a hike,
With socks that were pink and a dragonfly bike.
He pedaled along past the sleepy old trees,
Whispering jokes to the buzzing of bees.

In the echo, a gorilla replied with a grin,
'Why did the banana get lost in the din?'
They roared with laughter, their voices quite merry,
On paths that were twisty and often quite hairy.

A turtle chimed in with wise ancient rhymes,
Of distances covered, and very slow times.
But oh, they all giggled, for running's a blast,
When weight of the world feels too heavy to cast!

So wander the whispers that fill up the air,
Through valleys of quiet, let humor be rare.
For silence just waits, ready to play,
In the echoing stillness, joy finds its way!

Boundless Streams of Compassion

In a land where the ants wore little hats,
They coordinated dances with silly spats.
With a line up so perfectly precise,
They marched for the cheese—oh, that would be nice!

A cow found a hammock, took a long snooze,
While squirrels debated their favorite blues.
The sun beamed brightly, the sky painted gold,
While laughter erupted as stories were told.

A rabbit in glasses pulled out his flute,
With rhythm quite funky, he gave it a toot.
Around him, the critters began to shake tails,
A carnival spirit led all to prevail.

So gather your friends, forge bonds that won't bend,
With love that runs deep, and wishes to send.
In streams filled with care, let humor unite,
For sharing your kindness always feels right!

Footprints Through Fading Memories

In the park, I tripped and fell,
Chasing squirrels, it was quite a swell.
Laughter echoed as I hit the ground,
Those tiny critters, they scurried around.

With each step, I lose the track,
A mix of laughter and a snack attack.
Old routes twist in funny ways,
Just like my hair on windy days.

The bench where we shared our first ice cream,
Now covered in pigeon dreams it seems.
Each bite a memory, sticky and sweet,
While birds fight for crumbs beneath my feet.

Oh, the trails of laughter and fun,
Where all our adventures have barely begun.
Fading echoes of giggles, let's roam,
In the heart of these moments, we feel at home.

Embrace of Unseen Horizons

Off we go, into the unknown,
Maps are for nerds; I'll use my phone!
With every turn, we might go astray,
But that just means more snacks on the way.

The horizon laughs with a cheeky grin,
Chasing sunsets, we'll just dive in.
With ice cream melting down my hand,
We'll conquer mountains or a nearby stand.

Unseen places call with silly giggles,
While I trip over my own shoe wiggles.
Every stranger waves as we pass them by,
They think we're lost, and we might just fly!

But in every twist, there'll be delight,
Just a journey with friends, feels so right.
Let's embrace the weirdness, I insist,
Adventure awaits, with a goofy twist!

Heartstrings and Highways

Driving fast on these bumpy roads,
My playlist filled with the strangest codes.
Off-key singing, a real delight,
With laughter rising, we dance in the light.

Every highway signs a chance to laugh,
We speculate on cows and odd giraffes.
With a wrong turn, we face the absurd,
Squeezed in the back, I'm quite disturbed!

The sky above, a mix of moods,
Like my hair after some crazy foods.
Every pit stop, a giggle restart,
Fueling our journey, and warming the heart.

Dreams drift by in the rearview glass,
With silly faces, as moments pass.
Heartstrings tugged on this goofy ride,
Laughing our way, with friends by our side.

Tides of Time and Tenderness

At the beach, I built a sandcastle tall,
But the tide came in and took it all.
With each wave, I let out a frown,
But then I spotted a crab trying to clown!

Seashells scattered with stories told,
Of salty kisses and antics bold.
I stumbled over, my foot in a shoe,
While laughter erupted like morning dew.

With the sunset painting skies ablaze,
We prance like kids, losing our gaze.
In the tides of time, friendships grow,
Like goofy dances and silly shows.

So let's run wild, let the waves take flight,
In this whirlwind of giggles, we shine bright.
Tides may change, but we'll hold the cheer,
With swirls of joy and love, my dear!

Heartbeats in Untamed Wilderness

In the forest, I took a hop,
Tripped over roots, oh what a flop!
Squirrels laughed, they had a ball,
While I pretended I stood tall.

Bumping into trees, oh what grace,
Nature's playground, a silly place.
Leaves fell down like they would cheer,
My clumsy dance brought all near.

I chased a deer, or so I thought,
It turned to taunt, I was just caught.
With every new step, I'd misplace,
My dignity lost in the wild embrace.

Yet in this mess, I found some peace,
Laughter echoed, my worries cease.
With heartbeats wild, we all belong,
In this untamed space, where love is strong.

Radiant Paths of Connection

Stumbling on paths of tangled fate,
I waved to strangers, feeling great.
"Hey, nice shoes!" I loudly cried,
While they just stared, bewildered, wide.

Mapping connections, I must confess,
Each awkward moment, a fun redress.
We shared a laugh, it felt so right,
Two lost souls in the broad daylight.

Sidewalks danced under my feet,
Finding each step a comical feat.
In alleyways of chance, I tread,
Chasing after dreams, with laughter ahead.

As hearts collide in amusing ways,
We weave our stories, brightening days.
On this journey, joy is our song,
In radiant trails, we all belong.

An Odyssey of Silent Sorrows

I set off with a frown in tow,
Searching for joy, but where to go?
Silent sorrows walked beside,
Wearing their best, quite dignified.

Down the road, my thoughts did fester,
Until I tripped, becoming a jester.
A tumble here, a slip of fate,
Even woes can't resist to laugh straight.

Amidst the gloom, a chuckle bloomed,
As sadness danced, it was presumed.
We both agreed on this wild ride,
Where pain and pleasure do collide.

So here's to journeys, twists galore,
Silent sorrows, we can't ignore.
In each mishap, a lesson's spun,
An odyssey, together we run.

The Chorus of Serendipitous Steps

Marching onward, oh what a sight,
Each step a hiccup, stuff done right.
Feet in sync, yet heads do sway,
Creating rhythms in a funny way.

Bumps and giggles, all in the fun,
Lost my shoe, but never done.
With every twist, our laughter grows,
A chorus of joy, how sweet it flows.

Side by side, with quirks to spare,
Every misstep shows how we care.
In this dance, we find our beat,
Silly antics on the street.

As serendipity takes the lead,
We forge ahead, plant a funny seed.
With every stumble, we rise again,
In this lively step, together we gain.

The Lantern in My Chest

I carry a lantern, bright and round,
It flickers and wobbles, a sight profound.
It lights up my heart, makes me grin,
But trip on a rock, and oh, here we spin!

Bump into shadows, dance with the light,
My lantern's a guide, though it could use a fight.
It whispers sweet jokes, like a friend so dear,
Yet sometimes it flickers when I'm supposed to steer.

With every step taken, my lantern does sway,
It's usually a laugh, come what may.
It glows with my mishaps, my blunders, my woes,
A comedic companion wherever it goes.

So here's to my lantern, my favorite jest,
In the depths of my chest, it shines at its best.
Through laughter and chaos, I'll strut and I'll roam,
With my lantern in hand, I'll always feel home.

Serene Horizons and Silent Wishes

On the edge of the world, we all make a wish,
Hoping for fortune, or maybe just fish.
The horizon is painted with colors so fine,
But where's my sandwich? I left it in brine!

The sun sets like pizza, all cheesy and warm,
Yet my thoughts wander off like a stray little storm.
A wish for a muffin or a plate full of fries,
As the stars start to blink in the evening skies.

Serenity's nice, but can it serve snacks?
I ponder these fancies while dodging the cracks.
The moon's a big cookie, full of sweet gleam,
Yet my craving for dessert drives me close to a dream.

So, under the moonlight, I chuckle and grin,
Wishing for moments where laughter begins.
Silent wishes float through the soft evening mist,
While I contemplate dinner—oh, what have I missed?

Wandering Through the Veil of Emotion

Wander I must, through feelings so high,
One moment I'm laughing, the next I might cry.
With a hop and a skip, oh what a delight,
Yet every misstep gives my heart quite a fright!

Through valleys of doubts and mountains of cheer,
I trip over giggles as I shift into gear.
Emotions are like shoes, some fit like a glove,
While others leave blisters—good grief, what a love!

In the maze of my mind where clouds twist and twirl,
I catch a few giggles as my thoughts do a whirl.
With whimsy and woe, I'm a jester at heart,
With every odd turn, I'm a work of fine art!

So here I shall wander, through joy and through bends,
In the theater of feelings, laughter transcends.
With a wink and a chuckle, I'll take on the night,
Wandering through emotions, everything feels right.

Beneath a Sky of Hopeful Colors

Beneath a canvas, sprinkled with cheer,
I point to the clouds, "Is that a balloon deer?"
With giggles and snickers, I paint with delight,
Each brushstroke a shuffle, twirling in flight.

Rainbow-hued dreams swirl like candyfloss,
But sometimes, I stumble, my paint starts to toss.
A splatter of joy mixed with a dash of despair,
I chuckle while cleaning the mess from my hair!

The sky giggles back, in hues of pure glee,
As I dance 'neath the stars, feeling goofy and free.
With every odd cloud, I tap-dance and prance,
For beneath this bright sky, I'm caught in a trance.

So lift up your brushes, let's color the night,
With laughter and whimsy, we'll shine oh so bright.
Beneath this sky's colors, let us all play,
For joy is our canvas, and we are the spray!

Serendipity's Gentle Hand

In a café, I spill my tea,
Laughter bubbles, wild and free.
A sugar packet, bold and spry,
Danced away, oh my, oh my!

Pie in the sky, it seems so right,
Bumping into fate each night.
Chasing squirrels that steal my fries,
With silly joy and big surprise.

A stumble here, a trip down that,
I find the cat, who wears a hat.
With every twist and silly bend,
I find the magic in the mend.

Serendipity, my quirky mate,
We'll laugh together, it's never late.
With every mishap, we're a team,
Life's a playful, silly dream!

A Journey Beyond the Known

A map unfolds, but who needs it?
With every turn, I throw a fit.
Lost in circles, just like a pro,
I wander on, where? I don't know!

The GPS says, 'Turn around!'
I grin and laugh, not making a sound.
By paths uncertain, the sun I chase,
Accidentally finding a funny place.

A llama stares, judging my shoes,
I laugh along, what's there to lose?
Bouncing forward, missing the cue,
This joyful trek is all brand new!

Through fields of daisies, twirls and spins,
Every mistake, a chance to grin.
With silly maps and hearts so bold,
I'm off to see the stories unfold!

Whispers of the Wandering Soul

With socks mismatched, I hit the road,
A wandering soul with a funny code.
The wind chuckles, I dance a jig,
Every step feels just so big!

I meet a gnome on my way to town,
He tells me jokes, I turn around.
His beard is long, his hat's askew,
Together we laugh, who knew?

Through tangled trees and muddy knolls,
I find some shoes with glitter rolls.
Each stumble turns into a quest,
With every laugh, I feel so blessed.

So here I go, with heart in hand,
Whispers guide me through this land.
In each misstep, there's joy to find,
A wandering soul, carefree, unconfined!

Signposts of Love and Loss

The sign said 'right', but I went left,
A twist of fate, what a theft.
A love note crumpled, fell from my bag,
I tripped on a dog, what a gag!

In the park where laughter cries,
A squirrel steals fries, oh how time flies.
Sentimental hearts take a silly beat,
As I dance around, missing my feet.

From roses bright to cactus thorns,
Each patch of love has its own adorns.
With every tear, I find a grin,
Over faux pas, we all must win.

So here's to the map with bends and bows,
With signposts that giggle and play like prose.
In love and loss, humor we find,
A journey that's blissfully unconfined!

Unraveled Threads of Destiny

In a world where socks go missing,
I journeyed on, quite dismissing.
Each lost mate, a tale to tell,
Of laundry days and the wishing well.

I found my keys in the fridge one day,
My phone in the couch, just to play.
Maps made of spaghetti, oh what a quest,
Seeking solace in a pile of rest.

A cat with a plan, on a mission real sly,
Chasing the moon as it winked from the sky.
With every misstep and tumble I take,
Laughter erupts; oh, the joy of mistakes!

At the end of this trail, a cake stands so grand,
With sprinkles on top, just as I planned.
Now who needs fortune when snacks abound?
In hiccups of fate, joy is always found.

The Map of Yearning Souls

A map drawn in crayon for a treasure so sweet,
Leads to granola bars and a gummy bear treat.
With arrows pointing nowhere but down to the floor,
We stumble and giggle, oh, who could want more?

The X marks the spot, right behind the cat,
Who yawns at our plans, like, 'What's up with that?'
We skip over puddles, splash in our dreams,
While the universe chuckles at our silly schemes.

With backpacks stuffed full of snacks and delight,
We planned for a journey that stretched into night.
With each silly detour, our spirits soared high,
As we hugged every tree and pretended to fly!

The map ends in laughter, not gold or a throne,
For the best kind of treasure is friendship alone.
So cheers to our quirks and the joys we unfold,
For hearts that are yearning hold wonders untold.

A Voyage Beneath the Stars

An astronaut's dream from the couch, I decree,
With pillows as rockets, just you wait and see!
I launch into space with a cape made of sheets,
While dodging the dust bunnies, fierce little beasts.

The stars up above start to wiggle and dance,
As I twirl and whirl in my sparkly pants.
With a snack in one hand, I navigate wide,
To conquer the cosmos, let fun be my guide!

I found a new planet made of jellybeans,
Where gravity's low and the sunlight gleams.
But wait, what's this? A comet of cheese!
I'll take a big bite, if you please, oh please!

With laughter in zero-g, the night sings along,
To the tune of the universe, a playful song.
Returning to Earth, I float back to my chair,
In this wild voyage, joy floats everywhere!

Dance of Dreams and Pathways

Through paths made of marshmallows, we float and sway,

In dreamlike adventures, we tumble and play.
With laughter as music, our hearts start to leap,
As we pirouette past the ice cream, oh sweet!

A blissful parade of colors and fun,
With shoes on our heads, we spark like the sun.
We zigzag through rainbows that sparkle and shine,
With giggles that twinkle, we're doing just fine!

The moon drops a wink as we waltz through the night,
Chasing fireflies glimmering, pure delight.
With every misstep, our spirits grow bold,
In the dance of our dreams, true magic unfolds.

So here's to the journey, the mischief we share,
Where joy is the partner and laughter's the air.
In whimsical soirees under starlit skies,
We find that true wonder is just a surprise!

Language of the Unseen Journey

In a crowded train, I danced with glee,
Tripped on my shoelace, oh woe is me!
My coffee spilled across the seat,
And strangers laughed, feeling so fleet.

Whispers of socks lost in the wash,
With unmatched shoes, I'm quite the posh!
Got tangled in headphones, oh what a twist,
Even the cat thinks I've lost my sense of bliss.

A snail once told me to slow my pace,
But in my hurry, I fell on my face!
With maps upside down, I'm on quite a ride,
Yet, laughter's my compass, always as my guide.

So here's to the trips that don't go as planned,
Where mismatched adventures are carefully planned!
With chuckles and giggles at every little turn,
I'll map out the joy, it's my lesson to learn.

Echoing Memories Beneath the Stars

Under the stars, I wore my best hat,
Tied to my dog, who just wished for a rat!
We howled at the moon, that fickle old sage,
He winked at my dog and I flipped the page.

A kite in the sky, it zigged and zagged,
But I held the string tight, feeling so bragged!
The wind was a beast, with a mind of its own,
And once it took off, I was left all alone!

We tried telling jokes that fell without grace,
Like my shirt covered in ice cream, a colorful disgrace!
With laughter echoing through valleys so deep,
Memories floated softly, a treasure to keep.

So gather your friends, let's dance in the dark,
With starlight above, let's ignite that spark!
We'll trip on our dreams, as we twirl and sway,
In the world's oddest journey, come what may.

Lighthouses Along Life's Voyage

Paddling in circles, my boat feels like cheese,
It creaked and it groaned, I was lost in the breeze!
A lighthouse winked at me, 'Where's the shore?'
'In this sea of confusion, we're never a bore!'

The seagulls all chuckled, and took to the sky,
As I fished for my dreams, but caught a fly.
A crab joined the party, with a crabby old song,
We sang our off-key tune, it felt so wrong!

Navigating waves, with maps made of jelly,
I laughed so hard, I almost lost my belly!
The lighthouse keeper just rolled his eyes,
As I drifted past waves of laughter and sighs.

So here's to the journeys, both silly and bright,
With lighthouses guiding us through the night!
Let's sail with a chuckle, embrace every wave,
In this ship made of giggles, we're certain to brave.

Navigating Through Emotional Landscapes

I tripped over feelings, like puddles of goo,
With a map in my back pocket, yet no clue!
Emotions like roller coasters, round and round,
I screamed at the highs, and laughed at the ground.

A signpost for happiness? Oh, they're quite rare!
It pointed to ice cream, I sped with no care!
But found it was broccoli, in a cone, oh dear,
My heart sang the blues, but my stomach cheered here!

Navigating sadness, I followed a sigh,
It led to a cat that was waving goodbye.
But laughter erupted, just like a spark,
In the landscape of feelings, there's always a lark.

So here we go, through this whimsical maze,
With giggles and chuckles, let's set hearts ablaze!
Through ups and through downs, we'll dance without strife,
In the journey of feelings, we'll celebrate life.

A Tapestry Woven with Emotion

In the weave of silly tales,
My socks dance with great flair.
Spaghetti spills from my bowl,
And suddenly, I'm a bear!

Laughter echoes in the hall,
As we trip on each other's feet.
Like a clown on a roller skates,
Our lives are oh-so-sweet.

With yarns spun from laughter's grip,
We craft each twist and turn.
In this vibrant, knotty quilt,
So many lessons we learn.

So grab your thread, let's unite,
In our cozy, funny mess.
A tapestry of joy we'll make,
In this life we must confess!

Where Memories Blossom Beneath the Stars

Under the sky, we trip and fall,
While munching on popcorn glee.
Stars giggle as we try to dance,
The moon smiles back at me.

Ice cream drips, a sticky fate,
As we chase our own delight.
Your face is smeared with chocolate,
What a hilarious sight!

We pluck the stars and spin a tale,
Where memories bloom and swell.
Each blooper sparks a laughter fit,
Oh, this is magic we sell.

So let's toast to sleepy skies,
With stardust in our eyes.
Each awkward moment glows so bright,
As we watch the laughter rise.

Currents of Compassion

In the pool of friendly banter,
We splash with silly cheer.
Every word a gentle wave,
Making friendship crystal clear.

Hold your floaties, don't fall in,
Cuz laughter sinks those fears.
We paddle through the current strong,
With giggles, wipes, and cheers.

The tides of kindness pull us close,
As we drift on silly streams.
With every splash an inside joke,
That fuels our wacky dreams.

So come aboard this joyous ride,
Life's wave is ours to surf.
Together we'll glide in laughter's tide,
On this fun, compassionate turf!

Navigating the Labyrinth Within

Step inside my winding mind,
With zigzags and some bends.
A path of quirky thoughts I find,
With laughter as my friend.

I turn the corners with a grin,
As questions bounce and dance.
Lost in webs of my own whim,
Oh, what a comic chance!

"Which way to the ice cream shop?"
My heartless compass whirls.
But every laugh I spot along,
Is pure treasure that unfurls.

So let's wander through this maze,
With giggles in the air.
Together we'll embrace the haze,
Of joy beyond compare!

The Rhythm of Uncharted Routes

With feet so light, we dance on roads,
Our compass spins where wild dreams go.
A left turn here, a right guess there,
We giggle loud, not a single care.

Each bump and laugh, a melody,
A little detour, oh, can't you see?
We hum along the curious bends,
Maps are for folks with no good friends.

Oh, the ducks that waddle in our way,
Broccoli trees that laugh and sway.
With each wrong turn, we find new sights,
A treasure hunt of silly delights.

In this jumbled route, we find our groove,
With every giggle, we start to move.
Forget where we're heading, it's all a jest,
The joy in the wander is simply the best.

Footprints in Fluctuating Sands

In shifting dunes where laughs are born,
Our footprints fade with each new morn.
We race the tide and chase the breeze,
Building castles with mermaids, if you please.

Sandy toes and sunburned nose,
Jumping waves where the laughter flows.
A crab scuttles by with a sideways strut,
We giggle and chase, that little nut!

Seagulls squawk as if in jest,
Fluttering by on nests of zest.
With every grain stuck on our skin,
Another laugh, let the fun begin!

Oh, the tales we'll tell of sun-soaked days,
Waltzing with tides in playful ways.
With hats askew, and hearts so grand,
We'll still be laughing on shifting sand.

A Chronicle of Hopeful Hearts

With banners high, we march along,
Singing silly notes, a cheerful song.
Our hearts like balloons, ready to soar,
Who knew we'd trip on an old, squeaky floor?

Through valleys deep and hills so wide,
We find the laughter that we can't hide.
With every fumble, we cheer and shout,
Who needs a map? We're funning it out!

A wise old turtle joins our crew,
With tales of treasure, he claims to pursue.
We share our snacks, oh what a feast,
On this crazy path, we're never ceased.

When sunset glows on this misfit band,
We smile and wave, together we stand.
The quirks and quirks, they light the dark,
In this grand chronicle, we make our mark.

Sweet Serenades in Untraveled Lands

In lands unknown, we laugh and sway,
With songs of joy that chase fears away.
A squirrel mocks with a cheeky grin,
We dance with shadows, let the fun begin!

With every note that floats on air,
We spin around in carefree flair.
The bushes jiggle like giggling friends,
Oh, the silly antics that never end!

From mountains high to valleys low,
Our chorus rings as we wildly go.
With puddles splashing, we sing out loud,
Mark our territory, dance like a crowd!

In these sweet lands where joy expands,
We twirl and cheer, making our plans.
Together we weave our funny tales,
Living in laughter, life never fails.

Through the Lens of Warmth and Yearning

In a world so bright, we tumble and play,
Chasing our dreams in a laughable way.
With mismatched socks and hair that's a mess,
Our journey unfolds, it's nothing but jest.

We dance in the rain, with puddles so deep,
Splashing around, we find joy in the leap.
Our hearts skip a beat when we trip on a shoe,
Life's little quirks bring us laughter anew.

Embracing the quirks, we wobble and sway,
Each twist and turn, a new game we play.
With cookies for dinner and teddies for tea,
We're lost in the moments, just wild and free.

So here's to the laughter, in places we roam,
Together we'll wander, and always feel home.
Through giggles and hiccups, our spirits will soar,
In this banquet of life, there's always much more.

The Unseen Threads of Companionship

In a café corner, we spill all the tea,
With tales that make history, you and me.
The waiter rolls eyes, oh, what a surprise!
We're two hearts colliding, under watchful skies.

With jokes that go sidelong, puns flying in flight,
We weave silly tales into the soft night.
"Remember that time?" ignites all the fun,
Our laughter's the glue, two souls become one.

We navigate life like a game of charades,
With whispers of secrets and dessert escapades.
Your quirks match my wardrobes of hideous flair,
Together we're perfect, a comedic affair.

So here's to the friendships that dance in the light,
With snickers and snorts, all our worries take flight.
We'll laugh till we cry, spill our latte anew,
In this sweet circus, there's always room for two.

Portraits of Memories Yet to Unfold

With crayons and laughter, we sketch out our dreams,
Splashes of color in unpredictable streams.
Each scribble a story from days yet to pass,
We fold our adventures like a dress made of grass.

Oh, the selfies we take with our faces all squished,
The ones we delete, yet the laughter's not missed.
We'll dine on our failures, dress them with cheer,
Each blunder a canvas, painted bright and clear.

As clowns in a circus, we juggle our fears,
Balancing smiles on a tightrope of years.
From skinned knees to giggles, a tapestry spun,
Creating our future, our past just for fun.

So let's toast to the moments, however they bend,
For in each quirky twist, together we blend.
With laughter as memory, let's paint it quite bold,
A gallery of mischief, our stories retold.

Stars Guiding Starlit Souls

When twilight descends, with stars as our guide,
We launch silly wishes, oh, joyfully wide.
Each star sparkles back, with a wink and a grin,
As we dance in the dark, our mischief begins.

Under cosmic fabrics, our laughter ignites,
In the glow of the moon, we conquer the nights.
With spoons full of stardust and giggles that twirl,
We form a parade as we frolic and swirl.

The constellations giggle at our crazy prance,
Mapping our antics, we invite them to dance.
In each twinkle and chuckle, mysteries unfold,
Stories of stardust, in laughter retold.

So raise a wild toast to the skies up above,
For guiding our paths with a flicker of love.
Together we'll twinkle, a mess of bright souls,
With infinite laughter, the universe rolls.

The Journey of Unspoken Words.

I set off with a sock on my foot,
But somehow I lost my other loot.
Words in my head, like a cat in a tree,
I waved at the clouds, "Hey, come chat with me!"

Each sign I passed was a riddle or joke,
Drivers just blinked as I danced with my cloak.
Unspooled confessions on the highway's bend,
I talked to my shadow—my only friend!

The wind carried whispers I couldn't quite catch,
Stickers on bumpers, like mysteries matched.
My heart? It's a balloon—lost in the air,
Bouncing from thoughts, like I haven't a care!

A cactus I met said, "Don't rush, oh dear!"
He chuckled and shrugged, drank a cactus beer.
I giggled and chimed, "Oh, do tell me more!"
My journey was funny, who could ask for more?

Whispers of the Open Road

I packed a sandwich, forgot my keys,
The map was alive; it laughed in the breeze.
With a grin, I set off, my head in the sky,
Why do roads twist? I'm really not shy!

Potholes like drums echoed under my seat,
Each bump was a dance, I couldn't help beat.
Tires spinning tales of gum on my shoe,
Exclamations of laughter from a bird passing through.

A squirrel stole my lunch; why did I crave?
Was it for company or snacks I could save?
The whispers around me floated like song,
Who knew the road could steer me along?

With each little turn, I giggled in glee,
Adventure unfolded—just my car and me.
The open road's humorous, a twist of fate,
Let's revel, let's roll, before it's too late!

Echoes of a Soul's Expedition

I climbed on a cloud aboard a plush seat,
Echoes and giggles enveloped my feet.
Frogs in the pond croaked maps of delight,
So I hopped along, buoyant as light!

This expedition had blunders galore,
I once asked a snowman, "What's life at the core?"
He melted with laughter, a puddle of fun,
While I tried to figure out, "Am I the one?"

Worms wore top hats—what a curious sight!
In fields of odd creatures, I danced through the night.
Each step was a chuckle, a snicker, a rhyme,
Adventures written in the fabric of time.

The echoes of moments keep bouncing around,
As I tripped over dreams on the soft, grassy ground.
Seek not the serious, embrace the absurd,
Who knew that my travels would feel so unheard?

Beneath the Canvas of Longing

Beneath a sky splattered with paisley hues,
I painted my thoughts, what a whimsical muse!
My brush was a banana, the colors absurd,
Catching ripples of laughter that soared like a bird.

A squirrel painted stripes on a zebra's back,
"What's art?" I inquired, as it launched an attack.
With bananas as brushes, we made quite the mess,
Dropping giggles like crumbs, oh, who could guess?

Longing transformed, like a kite in a breeze,
It tangled and twisted, but never did freeze.
So I danced with my paint, made swirls in the air,
Underneath all the colors, there's joy everywhere!

The canvas was vibrant, a patchwork so bright,
Each stroke was a memory, a burst of delight.
So here's to the journeys that tickle the soul,
Let's navigate laughter, it's the ultimate goal!

The Cadence of Every Step

With every step, my shoes squeak loud,
I dance like a chicken, feeling quite proud.
Sidewalks become stages, my grin wide,
As onlookers laugh, there's no place to hide.

Twirling down streets in a tango with fate,
I trip over jokes, oh, isn't it great?
I leap through puddles, like a frog on a spree,
Life's just a stage, and I'm the marquee.

Each shuffle and skip, a mishap in line,
A waltz with my groceries, oh how they shine!
Bananas do slip, like they're part of the play,
But laughter's my rhythm and brightens the way.

So let's laugh our way, through the winds and the rain,
Each blunder a treasure, no need for the pain.
In this jolly parade, we dance evermore,
With heartbeats in sync, who could ask for more?

A Canvas of Forgotten Remembrances

Oh, the paintings of pasta that splatter the wall,
Artistic spaghetti, oh what a ball!
Each noodle a story, each sauce a surprise,
A feast for the senses, that dazzles our eyes.

In the attic, dust bunnies float like a dream,
They've gathered my memories, it seems they all teem.
Old socks tell tales of long-lost delight,
As I sift through the clutter, I find my old kite.

Painted mustaches, on family we cling,
With shouts of laughter, oh, the joy that they bring!
Each moment a brushstroke, so wild and so free,
In this gallery of life, you'll always find me.

So here's to the mishaps, a toast with a grin,
For the messier moments, that always begin.
Each spilled glass of milk, a work of pure art,
A canvas of laughter, that warms up the heart.

Threads of Connection in Nature's Embrace

In gardens we giggle, plants whisper and sway,
As weeds conspire, in their cheeky, sly way.
The daisies waltz under the sun's beaming light,
While the carrots are plotting a vegetable night.

Birds chirp in harmony, in zany karaoke,
Their voices a blend of both sweet and goofy.
A squirrel in a tux, what a sight to behold,
As he gathers his acorns, so brazen yet bold.

Leaves toss a party, with colors that clash,
While the roots hear the gossip, as neighbors they splash.
Every branch is a laugh, every flower a cheer,
In this crazy wild world, there's so much to steer.

So let's prance through the meadows, dance under trees,
With blossoms as confetti, swaying in the breeze.
Together we wander, in nature's embrace,
Threads of connection in this playful space.

Cherished Moments, Fleeting Echoes

In the hustle of life, I snicker and grin,
With socks that don't match, let the chaos begin!
Moments like fireflies that flicker and dart,
Each giggle we share, a true work of art.

The timer goes off, the brownies are burned,
But laughter erupts, as the lesson is learned.
With frosting to cover, we smile through the mess,
Each sweet bite a joke, baking's a stress!

Chasing the sunset, as it dances away,
Our feet in the sand, laughing at what we say.
Each wave that comes crashing is wild and loud,
Echoes of memories; let's dance in the crowd.

Through stumbles and tumbles, we cherish the ride,
With hearts full of giggles, our laughter won't hide.
These fleeting echoes, they ring ever clear,
Moments we treasure, my friend, you are dear.

Dancing Through the Storm

Raindrops fell like party guests,
Slipping on the muddy floor.
We twirled 'neath clouds, dressed in zest,
Laughing till our sides were sore.

Umbrellas turned to pirate ships,
As thunder clapped with glee.
We tightened grips on our wild trips,
Adventurers, just you and me.

Lightning flashed, a disco light,
We boogied till the dawn.
The storm may rage, but what a sight,
Our hearts danced on and on.

With wet socks and smiles so bold,
We stumbled home through puddles bright.
In every storm, a tale unfolds,
Of laughter, love, and pure delight.

A Mosaic of Moments

Snapshots of a silly day,
With ice cream mustaches wide.
We laughed and played, come what may,
With joy no one could hide.

Each moment stitched, a quilt of fun,
With colors that brightly clash.
We danced and spun, just like the sun,
In a whirlwind of a flash.

Spilled drinks became the best of cheers,
And awkward moves were king.
In all our laughter, shed no tears,
Each note made our hearts sing.

So here's to the moments, flawed yet sweet,
That make life a grand parade.
In every mishap, a joy we meet,
A masterpiece we've made.

Tides of Change and Growth

Waves crash loud, a playful song,
As we build castles of sand.
Each grain reminds us, right and wrong,
Change tickles, oh so grand.

The tide pulls back with silly swirls,
It's us against the sea.
With giggles turning into twirls,
We dare the waves to flee.

Shells collected, treasure chests,
Each one tells a tale anew.
Flip-flops fly, and laughter rests,
As we dance on morning dew.

The shoreline whispers, "Grow with me,"
We laugh, we stumble, we thrive.
In every wave, a chance to see,
The joy in being alive.

Heartstrings in Harmony

A band of fools with silly tunes,
We strummed our hearts so loud.
In mismatched socks and goofy prunes,
We played for a laughing crowd.

The guitar squeaked, the drums went boom,
Our jam was pure delight.
With every note, we filled the room,
Confetti soared in flight.

A chorus of giggles filled the air,
As we belted out our dreams.
To harmony, we had no care,
Life's a dance, or so it seems.

So here's our song, a quirky play,
With heartstrings pulling tight.
In laughter's arms, we'll laugh away,
Our music shines so bright.

Soulful Steps

With shoes that squeak and claps that cheer,
We dance through life, no need for fear.
A tumble here, a stumble there,
We laugh it off, forgetting care.

Like ducks in rain, we waddle and sway,
Chasing our dreams, come what may.
With cackles of joy, the world we impress,
In this silly parade, we jest, we bless.

In every misstep, a lesson to find,
With giggles galore, we don't mind.
Our hearts leap high, the silliness flows,
As we skip through life, in mismatched clothes.

So here we are, a comical bunch,
Sharing our laughter, loving our lunch.
In this grand adventure, hope does cheer,
With every step, we hold joy near.

Whispers of the Wandering Heart

A heart so bold, it takes to the street,
With a wink and a grin, it skips every beat.
Wherever it goes, a chuckle in tow,
It tickles the sun, puts on quite the show.

In search of joy, it stumbles and spins,
Dancing with squirrels, and making them grin.
A bear in a hat? Oh, what a sight!
Our heart just giggles, what a delight!

Every turn brings a mishap or jest,
In puddles of laughter, we find our rest.
The stars shine down with a knowing glance,
As we jive, jiggle, and join in the dance.

With every whisper, secrets unfold,
Adventures of warmth, both silly and bold.
Hearts paved in humor are always apart,
In the wild, crazy echoes of a wandering heart.

Echoes of Love in Motion

In the park's embrace, amidst giggles and glee,
Two hearts collide, oh, what a spree!
They trip on each other, a dance they have done,
Spinning around till the laughter is spun.

Each slip and slide a story to tell,
With ice cream faces, they cast a sweet spell.
Sharing their fumbles, their near falls, their plays,
In this circus of love, they pass joyful days.

As pigeons take flight, they altos, and bass,
Chasing down moments, they quicken their pace.
Through wild, wacky wandering, they find their ease,
Savoring love like it's a slice of cheese.

Their giggles resound, a sweet vibrant tune,
Under the grinning sun and the chuckling moon.
It's in these echoes, where wild joy grows,
In love's silly motion, life flourishes and flows.

Pathways of Tender Reflection

On pathways that twist like a curly fry,
We wander and ponder, not asking why.
With a hop and a skip, our worries are light,
Each turn brings a chuckle, as day turns to night.

In reflective pools, we see our own gaffes,
With splashes of joy, we share hearty laughs.
Each stumble, a treasure, each fall, a delight,
Playing hopscotch with fate, we embrace the night.

With love as our compass, we chart the terrain,
Our hearts beat like drums in the sweet summer rain.
In this merry adventure, where silliness reigns,
Tender reflections dance like whimsical trains.

So here we are, on this wobbly way,
Laughing our truths, come what may.
With every step, a giggle, a cheer,
On pathways of light, our hearts persevere.

The Land of Unspoken Dreams

In a world where socks go missing,
Lost among the clutter, twist and ding.
Dreams ride on the back of a bike,
Chasing squirrels with a grin, what a hike!

Giraffes wear hats while frogs play chess,
A dance party erupts in a giant mess.
Cupcakes sing, and juices rhyme,
All in this land, where dreams take time.

Rainbows sprout from pots of gold,
But who needs gold when you have bold?
Funny hats and silly cheers,
In this realm, we conquer fears!

So pack your bag with a rubber chicken,
Join the parade—it's time for kickin'!
Unspoken dreams can burst with glee,
In a land where laughter sets us free.

Collage of Heartfelt Connections

Gather 'round for a funky show,
With friends from places we barely know.
A cat plays poker; then there's a dog,
Making art from jelly and a fog!

A snail tells tales and wears a crown,
While penguins waddle in a ice cream gown.
Connections made in the funniest way,
Mixing colors like a child's play.

We swap our stories, both silly and wise,
With gummy bears mapping the skies.
Each laugh a thread in this quilt we weave,
A heartfelt mix—just believe!

So let's toast with juice from a rusty can,
To friendships bright and silly plans.
In this collage of absurd delight,
Each moment unique—what a sight!

Tides of Change and Reflection

Waves crash down on a rubber duck,
The tide pulls back, bringing much luck.
Reflections shimmer like jello in sun,
As we surf through life, just having fun!

Change sneaks up like a squirrel with snacks,
Stealing sandwiches and leaving tracks.
In the ebb and flow, goofy twirls,
We find ourselves in a whirl of swirls.

Every sunset brings another grand joke,
As the moon laughs at our little hoax.
Reflection can teach us to dance and slide,
With funny memories forever tied.

So ride the waves with joy and cheer,
Embrace the change; it's time to steer!
Together we'll float on this ocean wide,
In the tides of laughter, we'll reside.

The Alchemy of Place and Memory

In a cauldron of wobbly, jiggly tunes,
We mix memories like quirky cartoons.
A dash of laughter, a pinch of fun,
Stirring the pot till the jokes are done.

Places seen from a giant shoe,
With peacocks dancing in rainbow hues.
Each step we take, a story unfolds,
With memories that twirl like marigold.

Alchemy happens where laughter meets,
Transforming moments into silly beats.
Here, a cafeteria that serves up dreams,
On plates shaped like magical beams!

So wander on through this whimsical space,
Every corner's a smile, a hug, a face.
In the alchemy of hearts and cheer,
We craft our stories; the fun is here!

Refrains of Wandering Hearts

We packed our snacks, we're on the run,
With mismatched socks, oh what fun!
We lost our way to the picnic spot,
But hey, at least we found a lot!

We've danced with ducks, they quack and sway,
Accidentally joined a ballet!
Our map was upside down, oh dear,
But laughter led us here, right here!

With every turn, a brand new scene,
Stumbling through fields, so lush and green.
A tree branch waved, "Come play with me!"
Guess we found our true family!

Through silly selfies and ice cream spills,
We've conquered mountains and flatland hills.
Though tired and sore, we yell and cheer,
For every moment, we hold so dear!

The Journey Beyond the Horizon

Oh look, a car that's lost its wheel,
We might just need a bigger deal!
With snacks in tow, we stroll instead,
Chasing the sun, forget our bed!

Each step we take, it's quite the sight,
Rolling on grass, hearts feeling light.
We've set our course to the unknown,
With every giggle, our hearts have grown!

We met a cow who wanted to dance,
In the spotlight, we took a chance!
Though we are clumsy, we sway and spin,
Who knew a cow could join in on the grin?

With laughter bouncing beneath the stars,
Trading tall tales and wishing on Mars.
Wrapped in joy, with friends so near,
This journey's magic is crystal clear!

A Pilgrim's Heart in the Landscape of Life

With backpacks heavy and shoes untied,
We march ahead with hearts open wide.
Chasing rainbows, we take a leap,
Tripping on wishes, it makes us weep!

A squirrel stops by, it's stealing our fries,
We break into laughter, oh what a surprise!
As we stumbled through the forest maze,
We found a frog who wanted to play!

With every misstep, a tale is spun,
Bouncing down hills, oh isn't this fun?
Through valleys of laughter, we hum our tune,
Just wandering souls beneath the moon!

One final stop at a coffee shop,
Where tales unfold and laughter won't stop.
With hearts aflutter, our joy ignites,
Life's a wild ride full of quirky sights!

Navigating the Sea of Emotion

I sailed my boat with glee,
Through waves of laughter, oh so free.
But then a wave of worry came,
And now I'm just a fish in shame.

My compass broke, it spun around,
I thought I lost the joy I found.
But jellyfish brought a funny dance,
And here I am, in a sea of chance.

I tried to fish for hearts so true,
Caught a boot, what else is new?
With friends as dolphins, bright and bold,
We'll navigate this sea of gold.

So here's to laughs and quirky tides,
With silly hats and joyful rides.
Emotion's sea can be a blast,
Just don't forget, the fun will last.

Lanterns Lit in the Dark

In a world where shadows creep,
Lanterns giggle as they peep.
They shine with tales of silly fright,
Like ghosts that dance with sheer delight.

Each flicker holds a wacky dream,
Of popcorn clouds and ice cream streams.
When lanterns laugh, they light the way,
Through mishaps that make us sway.

Come join the parade of glowing fun,
Where silly stories just begun.
With every laugh, a lantern sways,
Guiding us through the wildest plays.

So let's light up the darkest night,
With every giggle, a spark so bright.
For in this glow, we find our mark,
And dance together, though it's dark.

Unfolding Stories under Moonlight

Under the moon, so big and round,
We share the secrets that we've found.
With winks and giggles, tales take flight,
Of owls who sing and bugs that bite.

I told the tale of socks that dance,
While frogs jumped in a funny trance.
With every twist and turn and twist,
We laughed until we could not resist.

The moonlight glows, a silver friend,
As stories twist and funny bends.
With every chuckle under stars,
We dream of worlds with quirky cars.

So gather 'round, let's tell our best,
With laughter, we shall jest and zest.
For tales unfold and hearts ignite,
In moonbeams we shall find delight.

Clay and Fire: Shaping Bonds

With clay in hand, we start to mold,
Our silly shapes, a sight to behold.
A wobbly vase, perhaps a face,
We laugh as our art finds its place.

The oven's hot, the kiln's our friend,
We toss in jokes that never end.
What comes out? A cookie, a pot?
Even we think, "Who knows what we've got?"

We shape our dreams with hands so small,
Creating memories, big and tall.
In fire's glow, our laughter flows,
As friendships spark and good humor grows.

So let's dive in this messy joy,
With clay and laughs, no need for coy.
For bonds are forged in playful ways,
With clay and fire, we'll sing for days.

Chasing Sunsets on Winding Roads

Driving fast with hair in air,
Sunset colors everywhere.
Dodging bugs and singing loud,
We're the quirkiest of the crowd.

GPS says, 'Make a U-turn,'
But our heads are flipped, we learn,
Roundabout's a dance of fate,
Laughing hard, we just can't wait.

Winding roads with twists and turns,
Who knew we would get this burn?
Looks like we're lost—what a giggle,
Maps or apps—they all just wiggle!

Yet in chaos, joy does bloom,
Sunset's glow, a silly room.
As we chase the fading light,
Our hearts burst with sheer delight.

Footprints on the Sands of Time

I walked on sand, then slipped and fell,
Who knew that grains could be so swell?
With each step, I lost my shoe,
Guess that's just what fun folks do!

Time ticks by, like seagulls fly,
Footprints fade, and seagulls cry.
Chasing waves, I dip my toes,
Only to shout, "Where'd my shoe go?"

As the tide comes rushing in,
I race the foam, a silly spin.
But in the flurry, I find grace,
For laughter blooms in this wild space.

Each footprint tells a funny tale,
Of fierce winds and an epic gale.
Life's a beach, just where I roam,
With sandy toes, I feel at home.

Embracing the Shadows

In the dark, a sneeze goes loud,
I trip on shoes, oh, what a crowd!
Shadows dance, they make me laugh,
Like a goofball taking a bath.

The moon's a spotlight for my show,
Starring me, the shadow pro.
I slipped on rocks, went for a spin,
Oh, the fun that's hiding within!

With every stumble, I find some charms,
Even shadows with open arms.
Laughing with the night so bold,
Turning all my fears to gold.

So here's to shadows, quirks, and light,
Who knew odd dances felt so right?
In the darkness, we'll embrace,
Every laugh and every race!

Songs of Resilience and Reverie

Strumming strings with toes in sand,
Singing tunes so poorly planned.
My off-key voice brings giggles near,
But in my heart, there's no more fear.

In this melody of silly sounds,
Every note joyously bounds.
When life gets tough, just play along,
Every blunder's a brand-new song!

Memories dance, oh, what a mix,
Turning trials into quick flicks.
We'll laugh and sing through thick and thin,
Reverie's where our joys begin!

So here's the anthem, light and free,
Songs of resilience, joyous glee.
With every note, we rise and twirl,
Life's a stage, let every laugh unfurl!

The Compass of Kindred Spirits

In a world of yum and glee,
We'll share our snacks, you and me.
With joy, we'll wander here and there,
No need for maps, just a good old chair.

With laughter loud, we'll build our dreams,
Pasta noodles and ice cream streams.
Together we'll chart this territory,
Every giggle, a new story!

Through kitchen chaos, we prance and skip,
With knee-slappers that make our hearts flip.
No GPS, but we won't get lost,
Friendship's the treasure—oh, what a cost!

So grab your snacks and a funny hat,
Let's wander far, but first—where's the cat?
With every step, our spirits soar,
Mapping memories forevermore.

A Cartographer of Heartbeats

With crayons bright, we sketch our fate,
A map of laughs that can't be late.
Each heartbeat's rhythm, silly and light,
Climbing trees and flying kites.

We'll chart the giggles, oh what a sight,
Every tickle-fight a pure delight.
With sticky notes, we capture the fun,
Like chocolate sauce on a warm cinnamon bun!

As we draw our route on sidewalks gray,
Tripping on dreams like children at play.
A compass spun by the friends we make,
Every silly dance, a map to take.

So let's scribble our trails in the air,
Paper airplanes zoom, with joy to spare!
In a world of maps, we're the stars that shine,
Cartographers of love—yours and mine!

Embracing Shadows and Light

In shadows cast by laughter's play,
We hide and seek in funny ways.
With moonlit giggles, we frolic and roll,
Chasing our dreams, that's how we stroll.

Haunted by echoes of silly pranks,
We'll dance with shadows, and give thanks.
With every trip, a story spills,
Our hearts aglow with happy thrills.

Under sunlit skies, and raindrop taps,
We wear our smiles like furry hats.
In every corner of laughter's light,
We find our way through day and night.

So let's embrace the dance of fate,
With shadows and smiles, we celebrate.
No heart too heavy, no spirit too slight,
Our journey's bright, oh what a sight!

The Silent Conversationalist of Nature

In whispers soft, the trees do chat,
While squirrels gossip, imagine that!
The flowers giggle with all their might,
In gardens where bees take flight.

Leaves tickle our ears, with tales galore,
As the rivers laugh and tumble ashore.
Nature's humor, a sight to behold,
In every rustle, stories unfold.

The mountains chuckle, standing tall,
While shadows play on the forest wall.
With every breeze that dances by,
Nature's secrets, oh me, oh my!

So let's tread softly, and listen close,
To nature's banter, which we love most.
With giggles and breeze, let's wander free,
In this chat with the wild, just you and me.

Canvas of Colorful Journeys

With paintbrush in my hand, I roam,
Each blob a tale of where I've flown.
From kitchen mishaps that turned to art,
To adventures where I lost my heart.

I stumbled on a rainbow, slipped on green,
A splattered canvas, a charming scene.
The hues of laughter color my days,
As trips unfold in the silliest ways.

Every shade a giggle, every stroke a grin,
As I paint my memories, pure joy within.
The world is bright, my colors bleed,
A masterpiece of fun in every deed.

So grab your palette, dance with me,
Let's splash the world in glee and spree.
For life's a canvas, let's fill it bright,
With every silly journey in our sight.

Notes of an Understated Trip

Pack your bags, but where's the map?
Oh look, I lost my way, what a flap!
With a snack in hand and a goofy grin,
Let's start this chaos, let the fun begin.

A detour? Why not! Let's explore the trees,
Humming tunes like buzzing bees.
With every step a misstep just right,
We'll laugh till it's dark and call it a night.

I found a pebble that sparkles like gold,
A treasure of nonsense, brave and bold.
My notes are scattered, much like my mind,
But who needs order when joy's what we find?

So sing off-key and dance in the rain,
A symphony of mishaps, joy, and pain.
In glitches, we flourish, in errors, we thrive,
Notes of this trip keep laughter alive.

Introspection on the Open Path

On a path less traveled, I tripped over shoes,
Wondering if chaos is one of my views.
With deep thoughts dancing around in my head,
A squirrel just nudged me; well, off I sped!

Each twist and turn leads to silence or chatter,
Like pondering life while I step in some batter.
I've questioned the path and where I should roam,
Yet here comes a bird with a song of its own.

I laugh at the wisdom shared by a leaf,
Dropping like confetti, what a comic relief!
Thoughts rolling like marbles, though scattered, they sway,
Each moment, a tickle, in my quirky ballet.

So roll with the punches, let quirks be your guide,
In laughter and musings, there's no need to hide.
For each stumble brings joy, like a playful fawn,
In introspection, my smile goes on.

Hidden Treasures of the Soul's Voyage

In the depths of laughter, I search for the gold,
But find only socks, mismatched and old.
Each treasure a giggle, a funny surprise,
Like finding a cookie right under the fries.

Navigating whimsies, oh what a quest!
With a map of my dreams that's a true humor fest.
I found a lost sock, it's a sight to behold,
In the treasure of laughter, our adventures unfold.

Buried deep in the sand, a rubber duck reigns,
A reminder of days filled with puddles and rains.
Soul-searching can jungle, fumble, and flop,
But laughter unlocks every strange little stop.

So gather your treasures, your quirks, and your cheer,
For every odd find brings us a tad near.
In this voyage of wits, let's have a great time,
Hidden gems burst forth in laughter and rhyme.